U.S.A. TRAVEL GUIDES

NORTH CAROLINA

BY ANN HEINRICHS • ILLUSTRATED BY MATT KANIA

Published by The Child's World®
1980 Lookout Drive • Mankato, MN 56003-1705
800-599-READ • www.childsworld.com

ISBN 9781503819733
LCCN 2016961186

Printing
Printed in the United States of America
PA02334

Ann Heinrichs is the author of more than 100 books for children and young adults. She has also enjoyed successful careers as a children's book editor and an advertising copywriter. Ann grew up in Fort Smith, Arkansas, and lives in Chicago, Illinois.

post card

About the Author
Ann Heinrichs

Matt Kania loves maps and, as a kid, dreamed of making them. In school he studied geography and cartography, and today he makes maps for a living. Matt's favorite thing about drawing maps is learning about the places they represent. Many of the maps he has created can be found in books, magazines, videos, Web sites, and public places.

post card

About the
Map Illustrator
Matt Kania

On the cover: The Blue Ridge Parkway winds through the Appalachian Mountains in North Carolina.

OUR NORTH CAROLINA TRIP

NORTH CAROLINA

What will you do in North Carolina today? Learn about the Wright brothers or learn about folk music? See black bears and hike up mountains? Get the scoop on pirates and race cars? Why not do it all? Just buckle up and start your engines! Follow the dotted line and hang on tight. You're on the fast track to fun!

WELCOME TO
NORTH CAROLINA

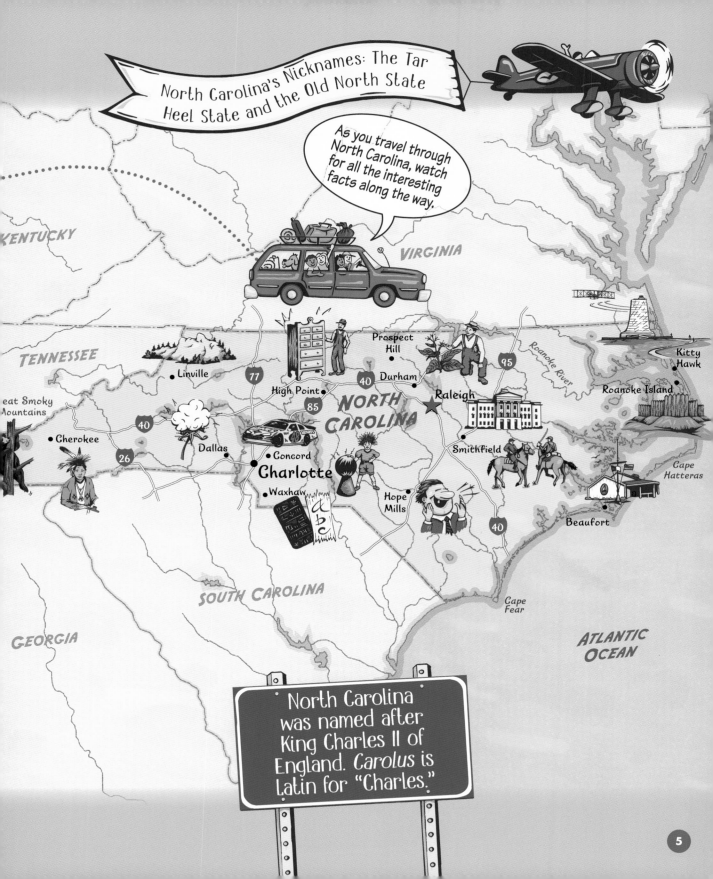

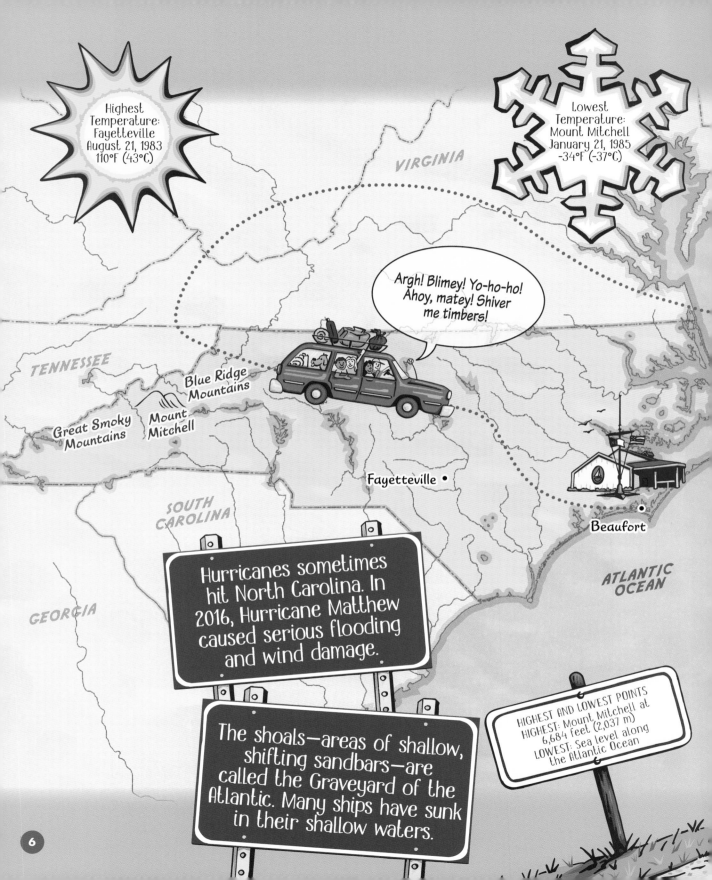

Highest Temperature: Fayetteville August 21, 1983 110°F (43°C)

Lowest Temperature: Mount Mitchell January 21, 1985 -34°F (-37°C)

VIRGINIA

Argh! Blimey! Yo-ho-ho! Ahoy, matey! Shiver me timbers!

TENNESSEE

Blue Ridge Mountains

Great Smoky Mountains

Mount Mitchell

Fayetteville •

SOUTH CAROLINA

Beaufort

ATLANTIC OCEAN

GEORGIA

Hurricanes sometimes hit North Carolina. In 2016, Hurricane Matthew caused serious flooding and wind damage.

The shoals—areas of shallow, shifting sandbars—are called the Graveyard of the Atlantic. Many ships have sunk in their shallow waters.

HIGHEST AND LOWEST POINTS HIGHEST: Mount Mitchell at 6,684 feet (2,037 m) LOWEST: Sea level along the Atlantic Ocean

Blackbeard was a fierce pirate. People trembled when they heard his name! His ship *Queen Anne's Revenge* sank in 1718. Visit the North Carolina Maritime Museum in Beaufort. It displays objects from the ship.

North Carolina faces the Atlantic Ocean. Long, sandy islands called sandbars lie offshore. They reach up to 15 miles (24 km) out into the ocean.

Mountains cover western North Carolina. The Blue Ridge Mountains are the biggest range. The Great Smoky Mountains rise there, too. They belong to the Appalachian Mountain Range. Central North Carolina is hilly. Rivers run from there to the coast.

Visitors admire a whale skeleton at the North Carolina Maritime Museum.

GRANDFATHER MOUNTAIN AND THE BLUE RIDGE PARKWAY

He looks old. And he looks like he's asleep. This rocky face is Grandfather Mountain. It "sleeps" in Linville along the Blue Ridge Parkway.

You'll love roaming the Blue Ridge Mountains. They rise along North Carolina's border with Tennessee. You can hike or ride bikes for miles. You might even see deer and black bears. Or try the Great Smoky Mountains. You can ride a train through the valleys.

The coast is another fun place. There you'll gather seashells and visit **lighthouses**. Look out at the rocky banks. You'll see why so many ships crashed there!

Grandfather Mountain is a popular destination for hikers.

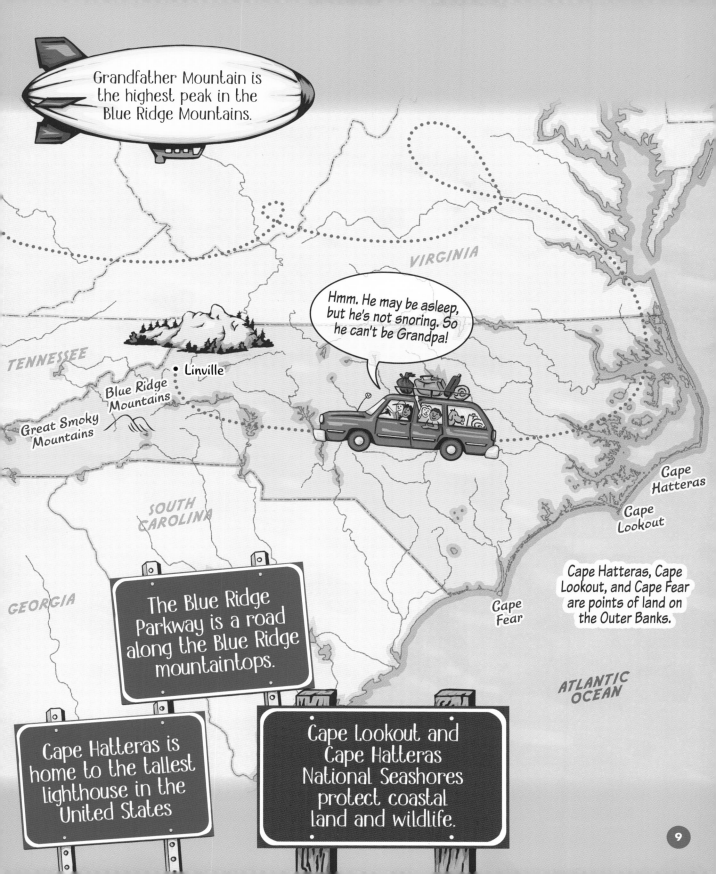

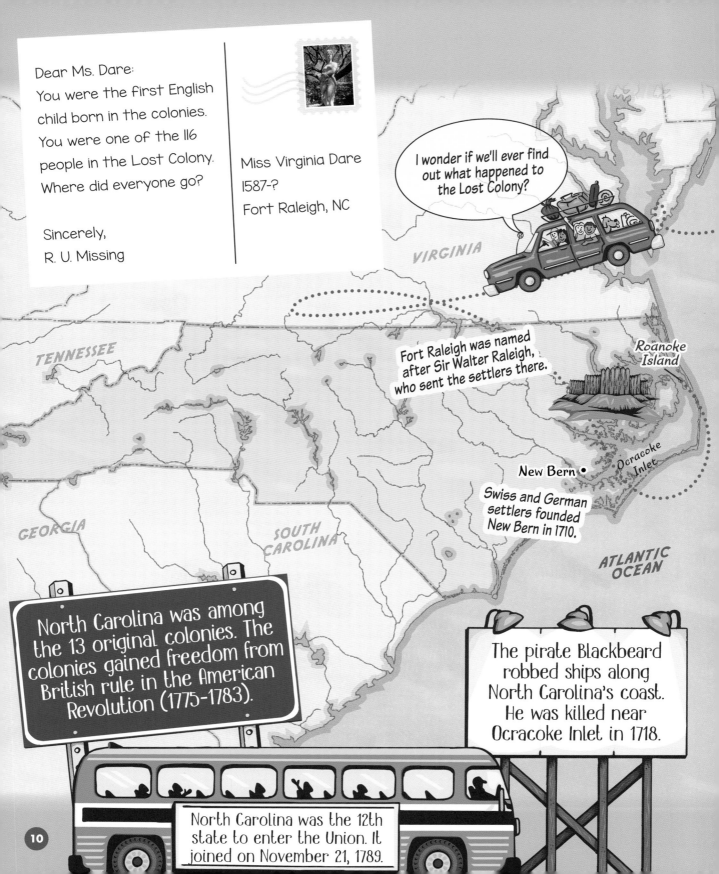

FORT RALEIGH AND THE LOST COLONY

North Carolina's first European settlers sailed from England. They arrived at Roanoke Island in 1585. There they set up Fort Raleigh. Life was hard in their new land. The settlers soon returned to England.

Another group came in 1587. Three years later, they were gone. There were 116 men, women, and children in all. No one knows what happened. They simply disappeared. This is called the Lost **Colony**.

More settlers arrived. They set up the Carolina Colony. It split into two colonies in 1712. They were named North Carolina and South Carolina.

See a replica of a 1585 English ship at Roanoke Island Festival Park.

OCONALUFTEE INDIAN VILLAGE IN CHEROKEE

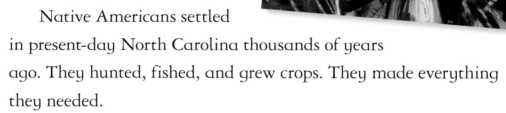

Explore traditional Cherokee houses. Watch Cherokee people carve canoes and weave baskets. You've stepped back into a 1760s Cherokee village. It's Oconaluftee Indian Village in Cherokee.

Native Americans settled in present-day North Carolina thousands of years ago. They hunted, fished, and grew crops. They made everything they needed.

In the 1830s, many Cherokees were driven out. They were sent to present-day Oklahoma. It was called Indian Territory at the time. Thousands died along the way. This journey is called the Trail of Tears.

More than 160,000 Native Americans live in North Carolina today. Approximately 14,000 are members of the Eastern Band of Cherokee Indians.

Participants greet each other at a powwow in Cherokee.

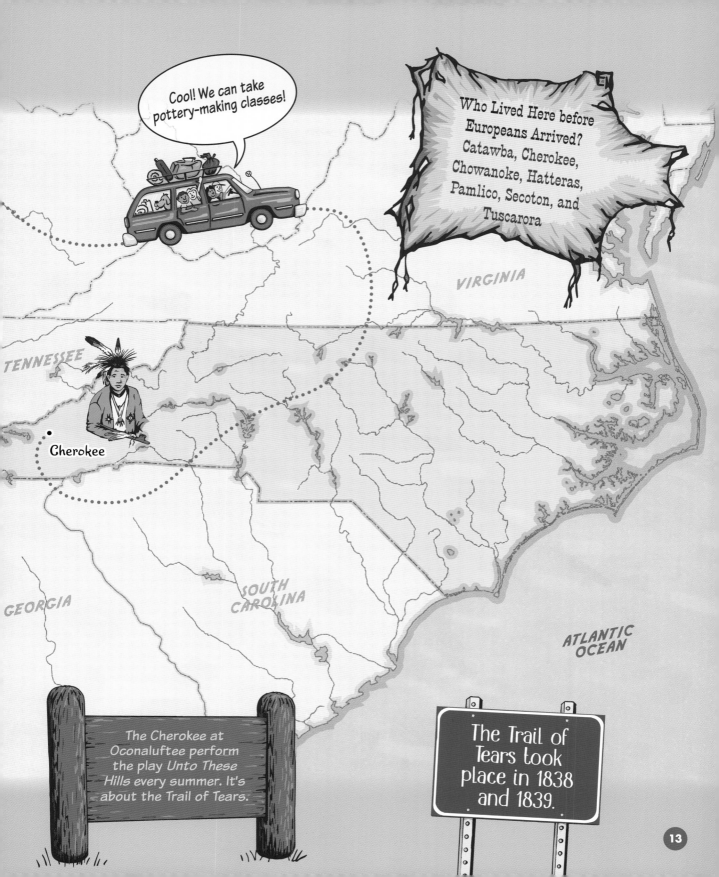

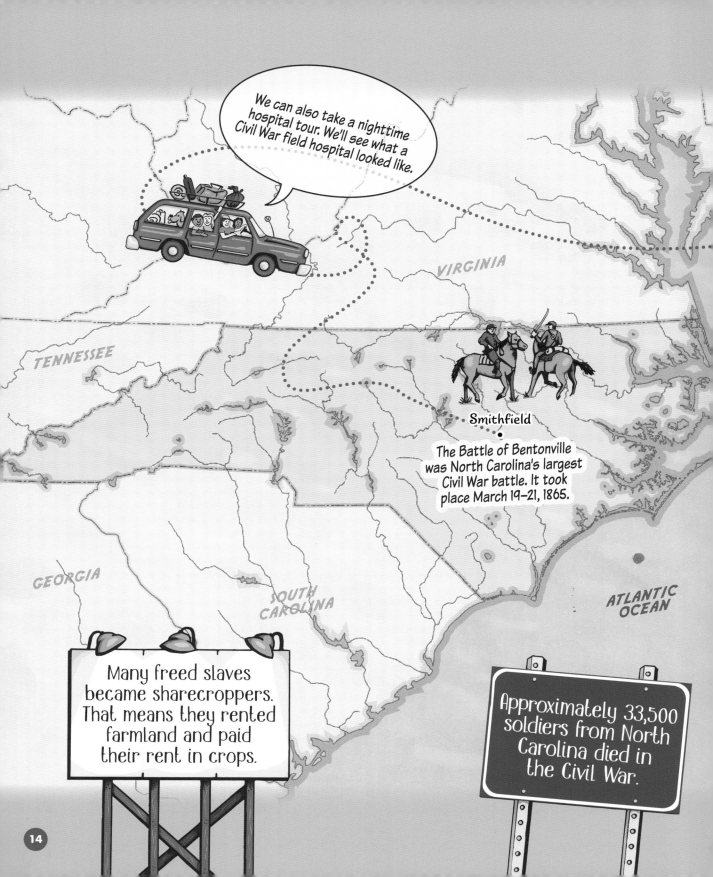

BENTONVILLE BATTLEFIELD AND THE CIVIL WAR

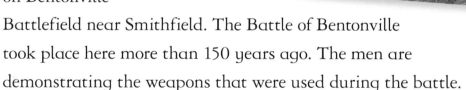

Boom! You hear the blast of cannon fire. Men in uniform prepare to load the cannon again. You are on Bentonville Battlefield near Smithfield. The Battle of Bentonville took place here more than 150 years ago. The men are demonstrating the weapons that were used during the battle.

Slavery was common in the South. Enslaved African people worked on North Carolina's plantations. These huge farms grew cotton and tobacco. But many people in the Northern states opposed slavery. The two sides broke apart. They fought in the Civil War (1861–1865).

North Carolina joined the South, or Confederates. The Confederates lost the Battle of Bentonville and the war, too. Then the enslaved people were freed. But it was a long road to equality.

See what daily life was like for Civil War soldiers when you visit Bentonville Battlefield.

Chug, chug. Sputter, sputter. Crank up those creaky old tractors. It's Cotton Ginning Days in Dallas! These old farm machines are the stars. They're more than 100 years old!

This festival celebrates North Carolina's farming history. Farming led the way to some large **industries**. Cotton mills made cotton cloth. Factories turned tobacco into smoking products.

Trees were useful, too. Sawmills cut up the logs. Then factories made wooden furniture. All these products made money for the state.

Is that snow? No! It's cotton. Cotton is one of North Carolina's top field crops.

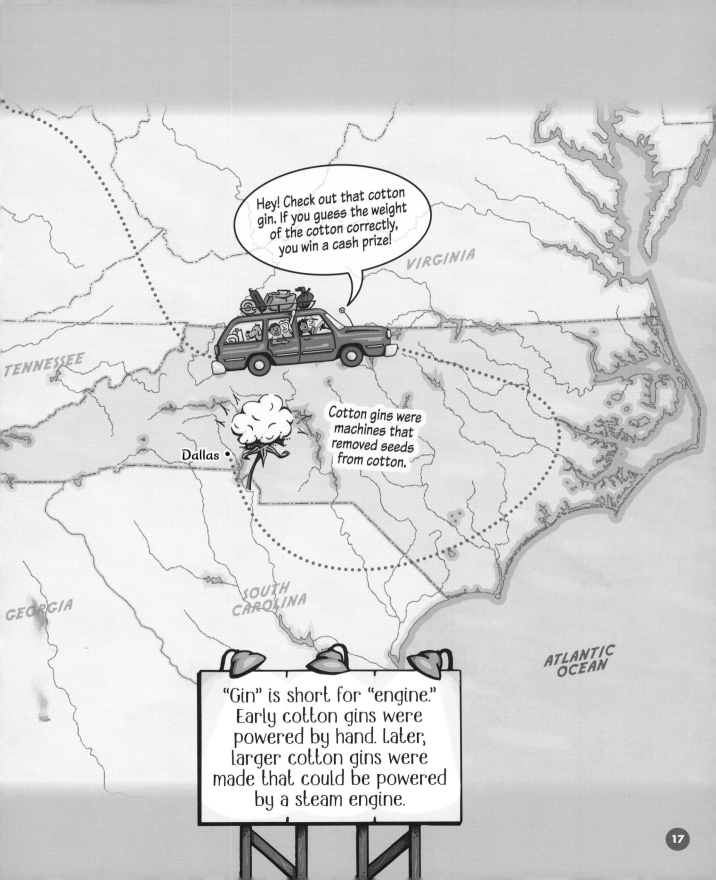

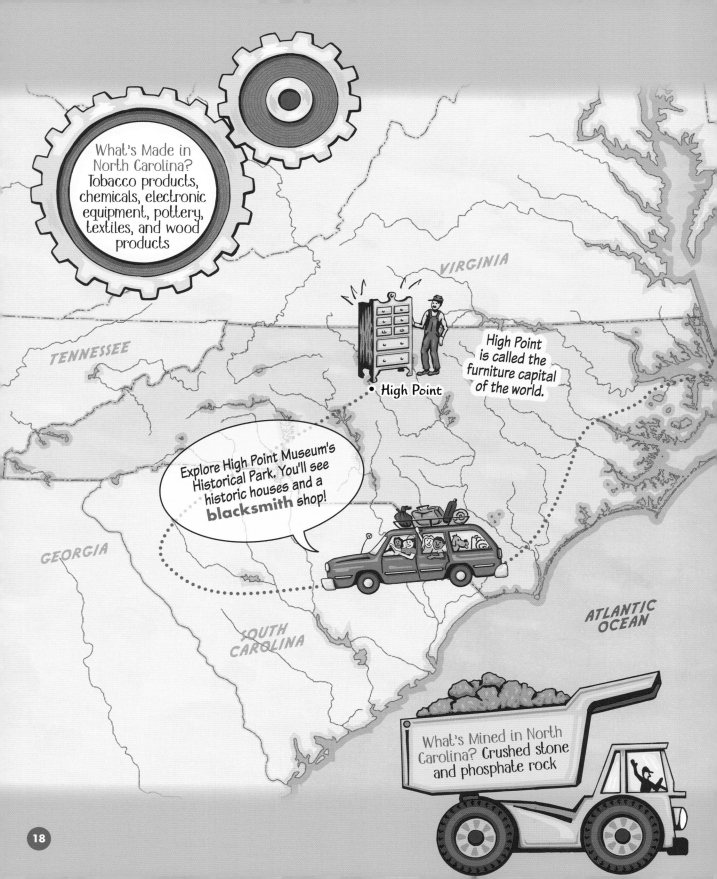

What's Made in North Carolina? Tobacco products, chemicals, electronic equipment, pottery, textiles, and wood products

High Point

High Point is called the furniture capital of the world.

Explore High Point Museum's Historical Park. You'll see historic houses and a **blacksmith** shop!

What's Mined in North Carolina? Crushed stone and phosphate rock

Want to learn how to make furniture? You're going to need some woodworking skills! Check out the Furniture Heritage Exhibit in High Point. It's in the High Point Museum. This exhibit celebrates North Carolina's manufacturing industry.

The High Point Museum is a great place to explore. You'll learn about different kinds of wood. You'll see hand-carved wooden dollhouses. You'll even find collections of miniature, hand-carved furniture!

North Carolina is the top state for wooden furniture. It's also the top state for textiles, or cloth. Put them together, and what have you got? A sofa!

How much work goes into making handmade furniture? Find out at the High Point Museum.

DUKE HOMESTEAD AND TOBACCO MUSEUM IN DURHAM

Top it, sucker it, and worm it. What does all that mean? Well, it was pretty hard work! That's what tobacco farmers did to their plants. Just check out Duke Homestead and Tobacco Museum in Durham. It was a big tobacco farm in the 1800s. It also had one of the first tobacco factories. You'll see how tobacco was grown and processed.

North Carolina is the leading tobacco state. Farmers started growing tobacco in the 1700s. Corn and peanuts are important crops, too. And don't forget the animals. Lots of North Carolina farmers raise chickens, hogs, and turkeys.

North Carolina grows more tobacco than any other U.S. state.

Duke University is named after a farmer called Washington Duke.

Some farmers hang tobacco in curing barns. Then they fire up a furnace in the barn. The heat dries out the tobacco.

VIRGINIA

TENNESSEE

Durham

★ Raleigh

The state fair is held in Raleigh in mid-October each year.

Topping means removing the top of the plant to control growth. Suckering is removing new shoots. Worming means keeping pests away.

SOUTH CAROLINA

ATLANTIC OCEAN

GEORGIA

What Does North Carolina Raise? Broilers (chickens), hogs, soybeans, and tobacco

What Are North Carolina's Fishing Products? Catfish, shrimp, Atlantic menhaden, and trout

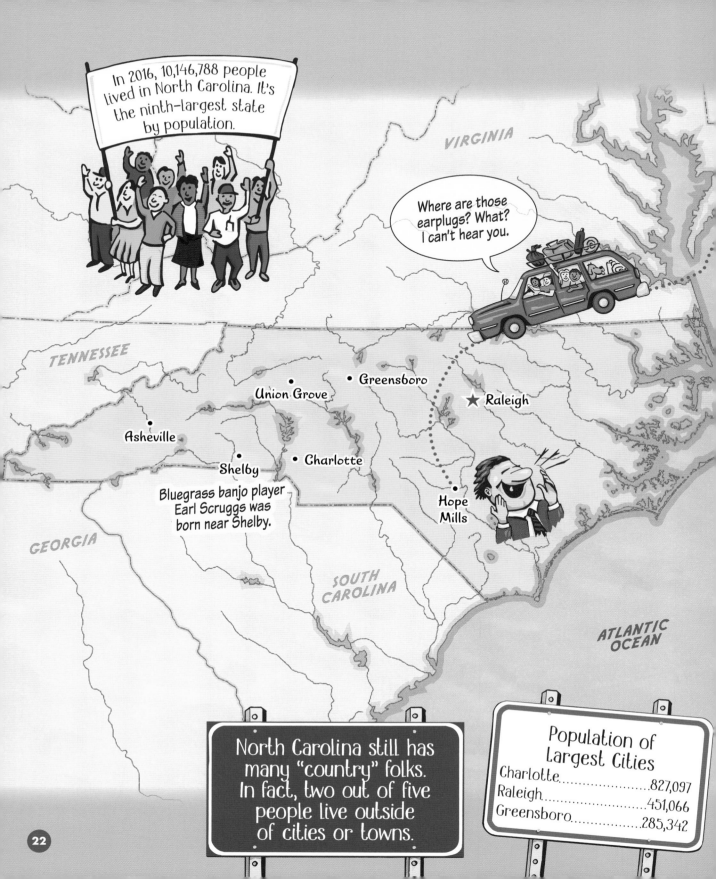

In 2016, 10,146,788 people lived in North Carolina. It's the ninth-largest state by population.

VIRGINIA

Where are those earplugs? What? I can't hear you.

TENNESSEE

• Greensboro

Union Grove •

★ Raleigh

Asheville •

Shelby •

• Charlotte

Bluegrass banjo player Earl Scruggs was born near Shelby.

Hope Mills

GEORGIA

SOUTH CAROLINA

ATLANTIC OCEAN

North Carolina still has many "country" folks. In fact, two out of five people live outside of cities or towns.

Population of Largest Cities
Charlotte..................827,097
Raleigh.....................451,066
Greensboro...............285,342

THE WORLD WIDE HOLLERIN' FESTIVAL IN HOPE MILLS

Eeee-OO! Yo-AH-dee-oh! What's all that yelling about? You've stumbled into the World Wide Hollerin' Festival!

This contest is held in Hope Mills every summer. It celebrates an old-time folk custom—hollerin'! Country folks used to yell across the fields. They'd greet neighbors or call for help. They'd announce dinnertime or call in the pigs. There was always something to holler about!

North Carolina has many folk **traditions**. Union Grove celebrates old music. It holds the Ole Time Fiddler's and Bluegrass Festival. Asheville presents the Mountain Dance and Folk Festival. You're bound to hear some hollerin' there!

Bluegrass music is popular in North Carolina.

CRITTERS IN THE GREAT SMOKY MOUNTAINS

Take a horseback ride through the Great Smoky Mountains. You'll run into all kinds of critters. The most famous **resident** is the black bear. About 1,800 of them live in the Smokies. The baby bears are really cute!

Chipmunks and deer live in the Smokies, too. So do wolves and mountain lions. They hide in the deep forests. Much of North Carolina is covered with forests.

Crabs live along the coast. Sea turtles nest there, too. You might even see some bears near the coast. Offshore, you'll see dolphins and sailfish.

Watch out! Black bears live in the Smokies. They're cute, but don't get too close!

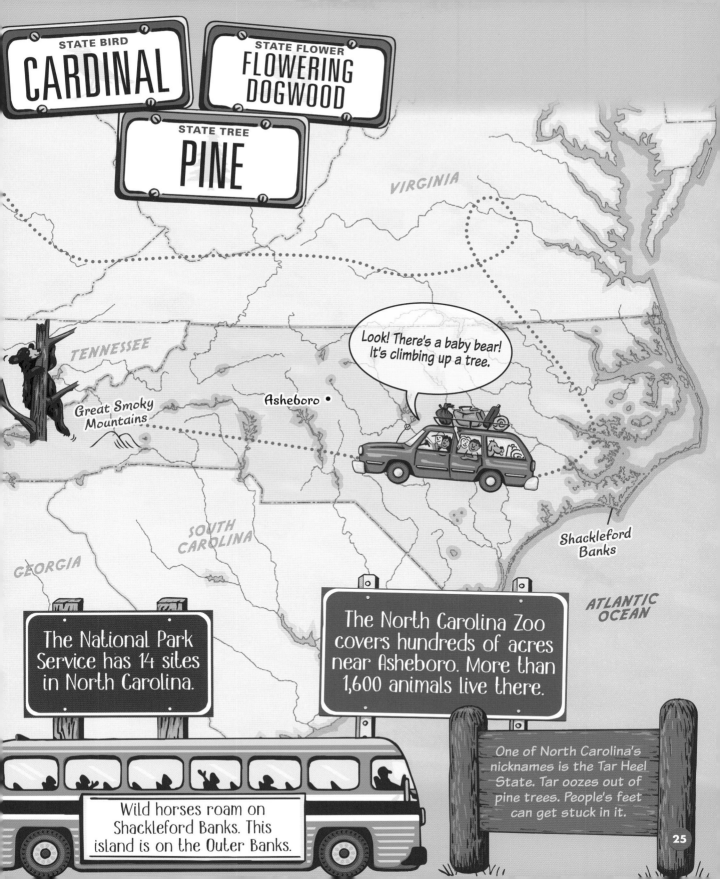

STATE BIRD
CARDINAL

STATE FLOWER
FLOWERING DOGWOOD

STATE TREE
PINE

VIRGINIA

TENNESSEE

Great Smoky Mountains

Asheboro •

Look! There's a baby bear! It's climbing up a tree.

SOUTH CAROLINA

GEORGIA

Shackleford Banks

ATLANTIC OCEAN

The National Park Service has 14 sites in North Carolina.

The North Carolina Zoo covers hundreds of acres near Asheboro. More than 1,600 animals live there.

One of North Carolina's nicknames is the Tar Heel State. Tar oozes out of pine trees. People's feet can get stuck in it.

Wild horses roam on Shackleford Banks. This island is on the Outer Banks.

25

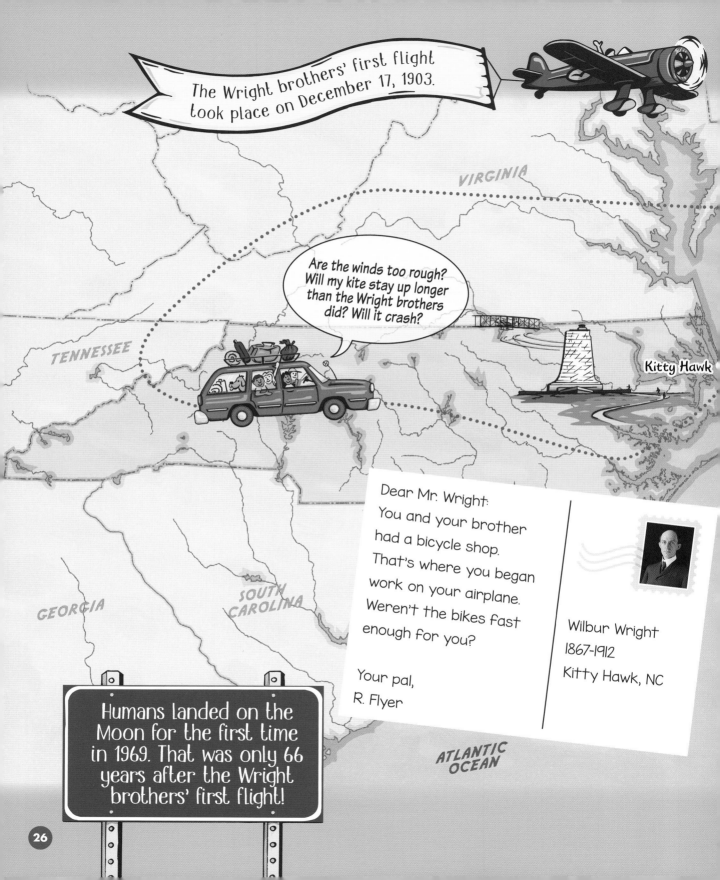

THE WRIGHT KITE FESTIVAL NEAR KITTY HAWK

It's off! It glides. It soars. And finally, it scoots down into the sand. You're flying a kite at the Wright Kite Festival!

Today, it's only your kite. But in 1903, it was a famous airplane. The Wright brothers flew the first engine-powered aircraft here. Their names were Orville and Wilbur. They're called the fathers of **aviation**.

The Wrights' first flight lasted only 12 seconds. They tried three more times. The last flight lasted 59 seconds. It was shaky, but it was a start. This led the way to high-speed flight—and space travel!

A memorial near Kitty Hawk honors the Wright Brothers.

DISCOVERY PLACE IN CHARLOTTE

Looking for a fun place to learn about science? Try Discovery Place. It's a science museum in Charlotte. One exhibit is a giant eyeball. You can walk inside it! Another exhibit zaps you with **static electricity**. It makes your hair stand on end!

Science is a big deal in North Carolina. Three universities lead the way. One is North Carolina State University in Raleigh. Another is the University of North Carolina at Chapel Hill. The third is Duke University in Durham.

These universities helped open a business and research center in 1959. It's called Research Triangle Park. Scientists there find new ways to make better products.

Learn more about plants and animals at Discovery Place Nature.

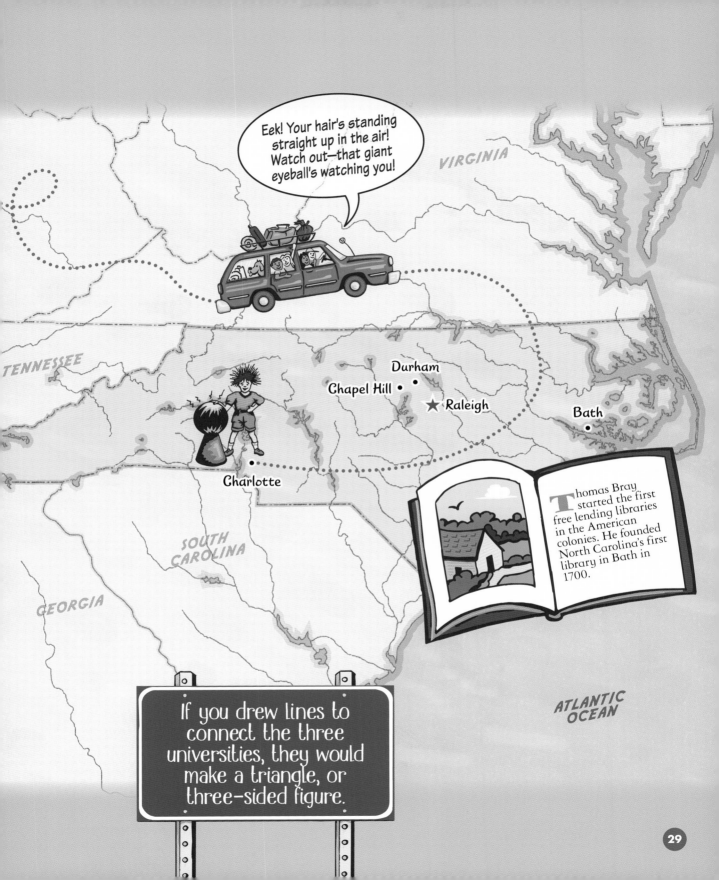

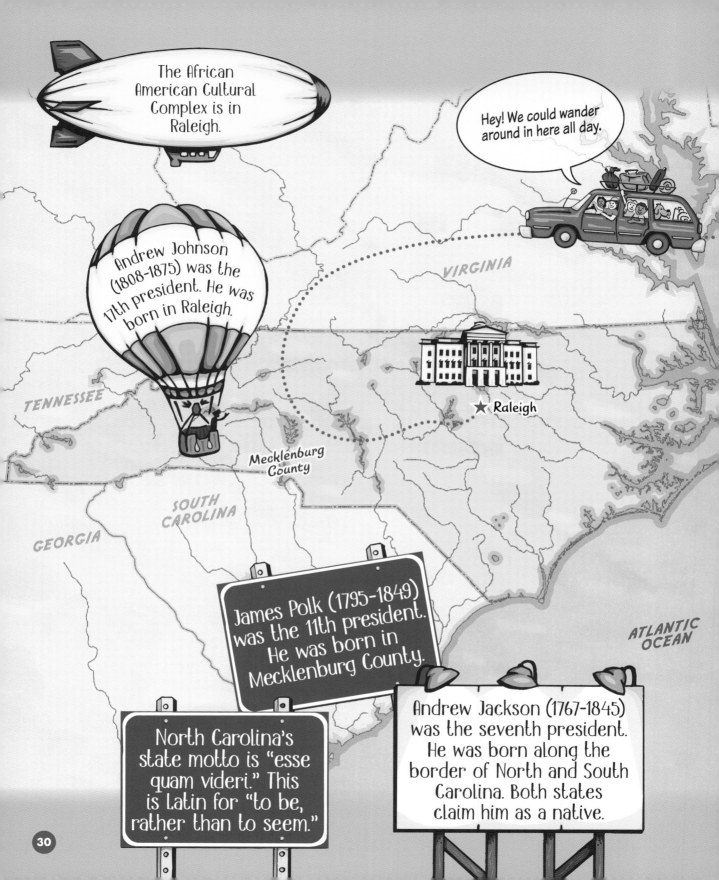

Is it a museum? Is it an office building? It's both! It's the state capitol in Raleigh. Some state government offices are inside. But mostly this three-story building is a museum. You'll see lots of fancy rooms with high ceilings. Some were once meeting rooms for lawmakers. One used to be the state library. And one held a big rock collection!

North Carolina's government has three branches. One branch carries out the laws. Its offices are in the capitol. The governor heads this branch. Another branch makes the laws. It's called the General Assembly. Courts make up the third branch. They decide whether laws have been broken.

The state capitol in Raleigh was completed in 1840.

CHARLOTTE MOTOR SPEEDWAY IN CONCORD

Vroom! Take a spin around the racetrack. See the pits where the cars gas up. You're touring Charlotte Motor Speedway in Concord!

North Carolina is wild about car racing. It's got dozens of racetracks! Charlotte Motor Speedway is a popular track. It holds lots of exciting NASCAR races. Those are races for stock cars. They're regular cars—just like the ones in which you ride. Only their engines are more powerful. Stock cars can reach fast speeds in a matter of seconds!

Start your engines! You're at the NASCAR races in Concord.

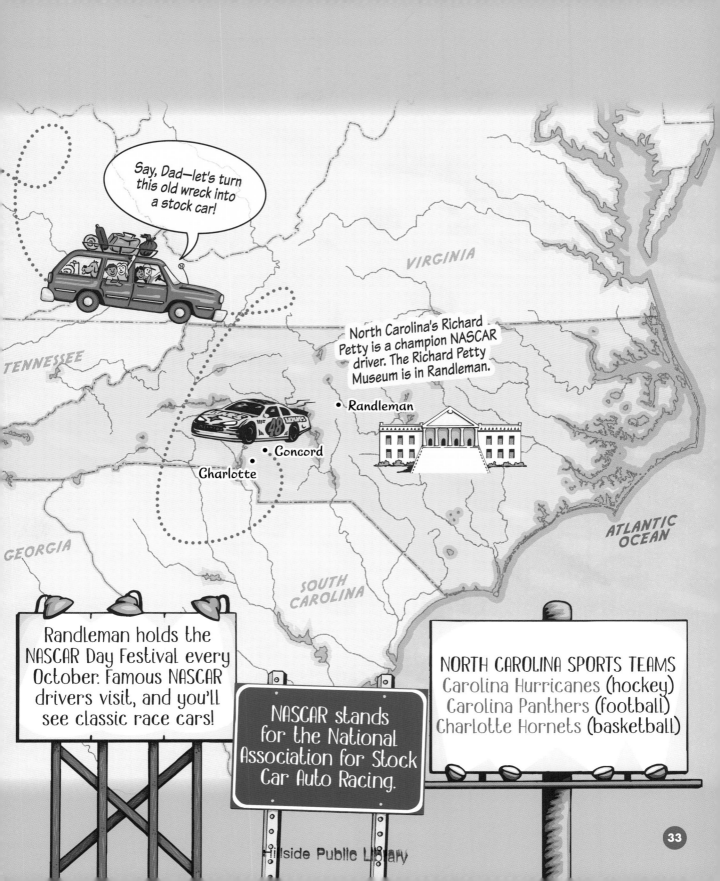

Say, Dad—let's turn this old wreck into a stock car!

North Carolina's Richard Petty is a champion NASCAR driver. The Richard Petty Museum is in Randleman.

VIRGINIA

TENNESSEE

• Randleman

• Concord

Charlotte •

GEORGIA

SOUTH CAROLINA

ATLANTIC OCEAN

Randleman holds the NASCAR Day Festival every October. Famous NASCAR drivers visit, and you'll see classic race cars!

NASCAR stands for the National Association for Stock Car Auto Racing.

NORTH CAROLINA SPORTS TEAMS
Carolina Hurricanes (hockey)
Carolina Panthers (football)
Charlotte Hornets (basketball)

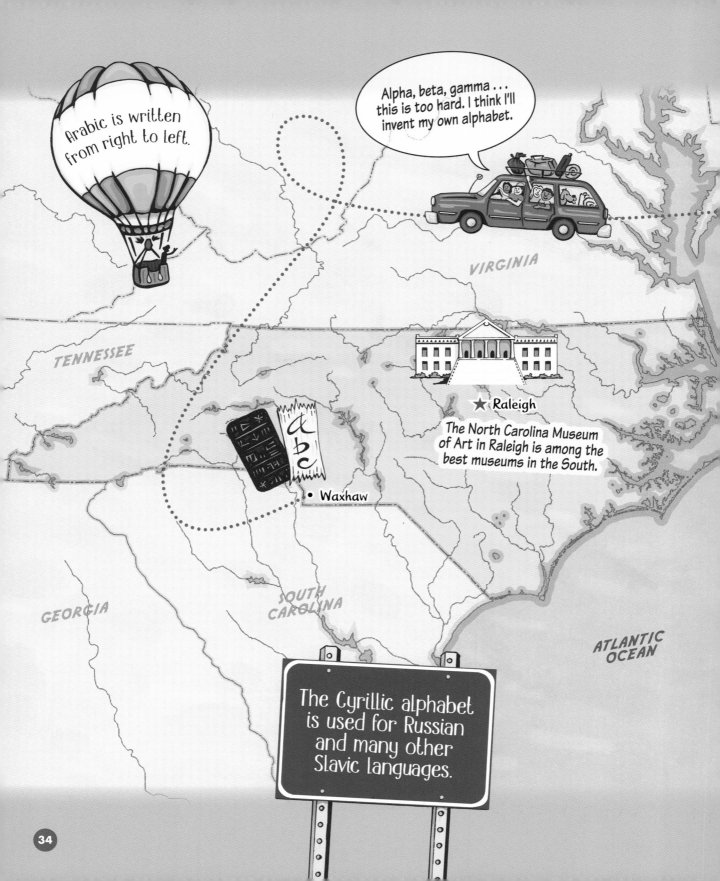

THE MUSEUM OF THE ALPHABET IN WAXHAW

Okay. You're a pretty good reader. And your spelling's pretty good, too. But what are α and β and ΩΠΣ? Don't know? Sorry! No spelling bee prize for you today!

You're at the Museum of the Alphabet in Waxhaw. It tells all about the history of writing. You'll learn about dozens of alphabets there. And you'll learn about the people who invented them.

What about the strange letters above? They're Greek. Start studying!

Learn about the Cherokee Native American language at the Museum of the Alphabet.

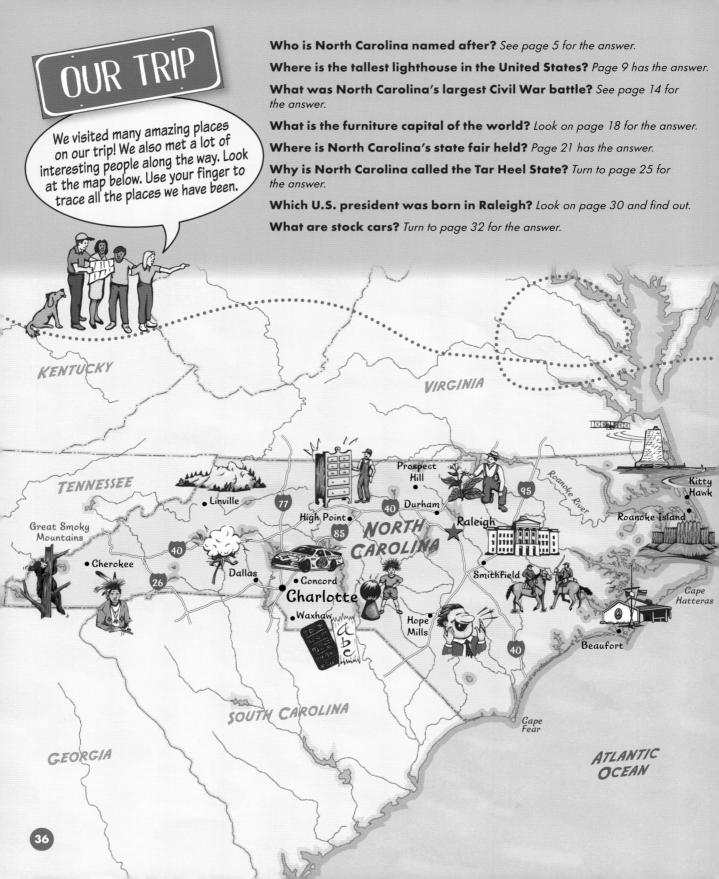

OUR TRIP

We visited many amazing places on our trip! We also met a lot of interesting people along the way. Look at the map below. Use your finger to trace all the places we have been.

Who is North Carolina named after? *See page 5 for the answer.*

Where is the tallest lighthouse in the United States? *Page 9 has the answer.*

What was North Carolina's largest Civil War battle? *See page 14 for the answer.*

What is the furniture capital of the world? *Look on page 18 for the answer.*

Where is North Carolina's state fair held? *Page 21 has the answer.*

Why is North Carolina called the Tar Heel State? *Turn to page 25 for the answer.*

Which U.S. president was born in Raleigh? *Look on page 30 and find out.*

What are stock cars? *Turn to page 32 for the answer.*

KENTUCKY

VIRGINIA

TENNESSEE

Linville

Great Smoky Mountains

Cherokee

Dallas

High Point

77

85

40

NORTH CAROLINA

Prospect Hill

Durham

Raleigh

95

Roanoke River

Kitty Hawk

Roanoke Island

Smithfield

Concord

Charlotte

Waxhaw

Hope Mills

40

40

26

Beaufort

Cape Hatteras

SOUTH CAROLINA

Cape Fear

GEORGIA

ATLANTIC OCEAN

STATE SONG

"THE OLD NORTH STATE"

Words by William Gaston; music by Mrs. E. E. Randolph

Carolina! Carolina! Heaven's blessings attend her,
While we live we will cherish, protect and defend her,
Tho' the scorner may sneer at and witlings defame her,
Still our hearts swell with gladness whenever we name her.
Hurrah! Hurrah! The Old North State forever,
Hurrah! Hurrah! The good Old North State.

Tho' she envies not others, their merited glory,
Say whose name stands the foremost, in liberty's story,
Tho' too true to herself e'er to crouch to oppression,

Who can yield to just rule a more loyal submission.
Hurrah! Hurrah! The Old North State forever,
Hurrah! Hurrah! The good Old North State.

Then let all those who love us, love the land that we live in,
As happy a region as on this side of heaven,
Where plenty and peace, love and joy smile before us,
Raise aloud, raise together the heart-thrilling chorus.
Hurrah! Hurrah! The Old North State forever,
Hurrah! Hurrah! The good Old North State

STATE SYMBOLS

State beverage: Milk
State bird: Cardinal
State blue berry: Blueberry
State boat: Shad boat
State colors: Red and blue
State dog: Plott hound
State fish: Channel bass
State flower: Flowering dogwood
State fruit: Scuppernong grape
State insect: Honeybee
State mammal: Gray squirrel
State precious stone: Emerald
State red berry: Strawberry
State reptile: Eastern box turtle
State rock: Granite
State shell: Scotch bonnet
State toast: "The Tar Heel Toast"
State tree: Pine
State vegetable: Sweet potato

State seal

FAMOUS PEOPLE

Angelou, Maya (1928–2014), poet

Barrino, Fantasia (1984–), singer

Byrd, Robert C. (1917–2010), senator

Coltrane, John (1926–1967), jazz musician

Earnhardt, Dale, Jr. (1974–), NASCAR driver

Gardner, Ava (1922–1990), actor

Griffith, Andy (1926–2012), actor

Jackson, Andrew (1767–1845), seventh U.S. president

Johnson, Andrew (1808–1875), 17th U.S. president

Jones, Marion (1975–), Olympic track and field winner

Jordan, Michael (1963–), basketball player

Junaluska (ca. 1770–1868), Cherokee Native American chief

Leonard, Sugar Ray (1956–), boxer

Madison, Dolley (1768–1849), first lady

Monk, Thelonious (1917–1982), jazz musician

Paul, Chris (1985–), basketball player

Polk, James K. (1795–1849), 11th U.S. president

Porter, William Sydney (O. Henry) (1862–1910), author

Scruggs, Earl (1924–2012), bluegrass musician

Simone, Nina (1933–2003), singer

WORDS TO KNOW

aviation (ay-vee-AY-shuhn) constructing and flying airplanes

blacksmith (BLAK-smith) someone who makes metal objects using fire to heat the metal and a hammer to shape it

colony (KOL-uh-nee) a new land settled by people from another country

industries (IN-duh-streez) types of businesses

lighthouses (LITE-houss-ez) tall, thin buildings with a bright light on top to warn ships that they are near shore

resident (REZ-uh-duhnt) someone or something living in a certain place

static electricity (STAT-ik ee-lek-TRISS-uh-tee) electrical energy produced by rubbing two objects together

traditions (truh-DISH-uhnz) customs handed down over many years

State flag

TO LEARN MORE

IN THE LIBRARY

Cunningham, Kevin. *The North Carolina Colony.* New York, NY: Children's Press, 2012.

Hunt, Santana. *Great Smoky Mountains National Park.* New York, NY: Gareth Stevens, 2016.

Sweazey, Davy. *North Carolina: The Tar Heel State.* Minneapolis, MN: Bellwether, 2014.

Zardes, Cassandra. *Cherokee.* New York, NY: PowerKids Press, 2016.

ON THE WEB

Visit our Web site for links about North Carolina:
childsworld.com/links

Note to Parents, Teachers, and Librarians: We routinely verify our Web links to make sure they are safe and active sites. So encourage your readers to check them out!

PLACES TO VISIT OR CONTACT

North Carolina Tourism
visitnc.com
301 North Wilmington Street
Raleigh, NC 27601
800/847-4862
For more information about traveling in North Carolina

North Carolina Museum of History
ncmuseumofhistory.org
5 East Edenton Street
Raleigh, NC 27601
919/807-7900
For more information about the history of North Carolina

North Carolina covers 53,819 square miles (139,391 sq km). It's the 28th-largest state in size.

INDEX

Bye, Old North State.
We had a great time.
We'll come back soon!